detour

Also by Nancy White

Sun, Moon, Salt

detour

poems by

Nancy White

Tamarack Editions

Published by Tamarack Editions, LLC
P.O. Box 523
Penns Park, PA 18943-0523

On the web at www.tamarackeditions.net

Typeset in Palatino Linotype
with Franklin Gothic Heavy display

ISBN 978-0-9796684-3-2
LCCN: 2009933927

Cover design by Allen Hoey
Stock photo

Labor donated

acknowledgments

The author grateful for the support of the following journals in which some of these poems originally appeared.

Antioch Review: "Grasslands"; *Beloit Poetry Journal*: "Man Overboard"; *Black Warrior Review*: "Five Fantastic Ways to Die"; *California Quarterly*: "Tide Going Out"; *Chautauqua Literary Journal*: "Paradise"; *Cincinnati Review*: "Beauty"; *Colorado Review*: "The Porch"; *Confrontation*: "Pocket"; *Cottonwood*: "Green"; *Descant*: "With Baptized Eyes"; *Diner*: "He Learns to Speak" and "The Drinkers"; *Feminist Studies*: "The Wonder"; *FIELD*: "Your Mother Starts Speaking," "The Water Said," and "Summer"; *Free Lunch*: "Wives"; *Fugue*: "Look Up"; *The Nebraska Review*: "Through the Wall a Voice"; *New Letters*: "Woven and Sewn" & "Ceremony for Coming of Age"; *New Orphic Review*: "You Cannot Say" and "They Ask You about Middle Age"; *New Zoo Poetry Review*: "Blue Torso"; *Nimrod*: "Steps to Hell," & "Other Girl"; *Pebble Lake Review*: "The Owl in Your Name"; *Phoebe*: "Five Sure-Fire Steps for Rescue" and "What Happened"; *Ploughshares*: "We Look Back and See" (as "Man"); *Poet Lore*: "Below the Lifeboat"; *Porcupine*: "Yes No" and "Propeller"; *Rattle*: "The Body"; *Rhino*: "Girl Who Liked Doors"; *Salt Hill*: "Your Life Has Stood" and "What You Should Say When He Asks"; *Stand*: "Divorce Comedy"; *Virginia Quarterly Review*: "Asthma"; and *Washington Square*: "Thirst."

for the crones

contents

3 no sequel   51

1

smoke

woven and sewn

You are no virgin listen. You must stop here.

Sit on the curb and look like a bum.

Hold still until you feel it too.

There is a *no* rising in you like clear sap like power.

Do not drill in your side. The world is not asking for this.

You are meant to stream upwards. No compromise only pause.

Sit in the dirt of the road until you see.

If it takes years it takes years.

This will cost less than the life you would drain from your side.

If you are hungry sleepless cold it is nothing to the other suffering.

There is no such *have to* that lie.

We once told it too. Don't be ashamed.

You are part of this fabric woven and sewn.

But not this what you contemplate willingly today.

You may hate us for these words. It passes.

Believe you are the one in danger. Sit down.

beauty

his copper hair his forearm glossy softening
waist scrotum rough his suddenly
attentive kiss his

monstrous appetite for meat his
whims analyzed and deified his hilarity
with children his tin voice his pursed

lips his backbeat rhythm his sigh when
he comes when he takes the first bite
his legs in black his tough rust

colored nipples his neck smelling of
narcissus his lack of hangnails his laugh like
a landmine such intention

of goodness his appearance golden his
tantrums his silence frozen after fine sex
cordial after bad his beauty his

beauty his darkness is love

propeller

trees like water stirred
by a wide propeller   anchored like a tongue
plump grub he surges   real

in his pod   your heart shudders
thuds   afraid to pause
coming down   a mountain road too fast

you are to   eat more meat   noticing what
does and   doesn't last   noticing you could
do none   of this on purpose   trees thrash

as if to climb   out of their roots and
you don't know   don't know
because all of this   so far is   mostly made of fear

you didn't

need the word
you had his bent-hazel
mind and belly of sorrow

didn't need the glance of god
or vow past this
but then his face his

musically atonal
delay grew (he explained)
sacred page one new

story you thought we stayed
mortal got supple &
plain like fine shoes

hadn't said swear
didn't want need
only free continuance

not his name

your father, your son

He carved the dusk with stories—his trick
to dive with lit cigarette and come up smoking,
or the girl he danced with late, her brothers
interrupting with a gun—but he never much

listened to you, no matter how you guzzled
his gruff heat, the musk of his overalls, the fine foul
language of his big male freedom. Four daughters,
no sons. He was all you had, so he's still the man

to turn to, saying *You took the dog in the boat not us.*
You stayed late with the neighbors, called us liars,
didn't care if we walked in the road. In you now
a bud, a son who will rise like weather,

poured from your genuine, unnamed ore, from his
genuine, unnamed ore. You say this one
won't taste the blade that separates love
from its genderless shape. You swear it.

sensualist on hold

Such delays,
costly, mix

(the rest of) us
with the prurient or
resigned. Don't

wait, don't
monitor for pulse—(again)

alive in the lips hips
dialogue dig (buzz and
hub)—saliva—our

taste *above* dear. Hear
us, hear us, the mere?

what you are waiting for

affordable fate to come like a hawk
diving from the sky

to give up spices
live clean by the edge of the pit and

forget how the fiend cradled
your pillows so yellow and blue

to ignore the usual suspects
yet no avalanche reckons your spine

for your breath and our breath to walk
the earth and find what these lungs are for

boy dream

Nested like a housewife's mixing bowls, rocking: three men
and you. Light slides on you jealously,
croons *please please* as you tip, china-fine as egg-
shells. The moon gorges on your milky rims, divides
like silk across the bow of each man's back.
You are the inside and in you the plum, anchored
by his tough blue stem, multiplies, rides
the muttering tide as the men suck the palms
of your feet and hands, as they lick the sides
of your face. Now: enough
men. Jim swarming
against Jacob's velvet ass as
Jon nuzzles the stubble along
Jake's jaw and slow as
Gregorian chant eases
his thumb deeper
into Jim while Jake
sucks on the pads
of fingers and sinks
himself into the
pillow and surge of
man. They're pungency
and urgency and wear
the smile of sleep
all over their bodies, men, the plush
push of them. They drink bitter, drink sour,

love all the lovers of men, all ways men love.
Three cupping you like the meaty petals of the lily,
smelling dune-grass, clove, sweat from the father's
groin, and they furl from you, roll back from the sta-
men crucial and long like shots of light riding down
the throat of the thirsty world. You're the shaft to
arc to, and the meteor shivering at the tip, swollen,
bold, is your child, the boy, rising as your new
word when you arrive together knowing *yes*.

thirst

you watch bubbles cling to the luminous side
of the glass   a fiery scarf of bubbles the glass wears outside
its water   inside itself   you haven't made love much

lately   the baby takes over circuits and you are afraid
of being tired   of being two tired people and so you save
yourselves   for the baby   for later   for the sake

of cheerfulness and conversation   one silver bubble slips and
as if plucked detaches   sails up the column of bright
water   a tiny knuckle knocking another as it

lifts past so it too skips
its moorings   glides away from the silky glass   rises and
after a pause one more lets go   then two   flying

and such speed-pearls they cut
toward the sky and you want   you
think about   reaching over and rapping the glass   no

you'd raise and slam it so all those bubble hundreds
lose their heads and
burst up for the sun the air the light and go

the water said

It didn't matter, didn't mean anything. Too much
hair, he says, and flesh, and cigarettes. He was

drunk. She tasted bad. He thinks she faked it. Just
what has appeared to be your life lifted from your hands

and spilling, a little. You lie at the bottom, a still,
speeding place. Of the cold like a trout, of the silence

behind motion, you are less than the fish. But it waits
for you—honey-colored shed, new timing belt, a fly with eyes

like green fire—back in the air. You let go of the bottom where
dead things roll and the light breaks back into your lungs.

honest

let's be
honest you do not
like him the way he
is and he does not like you yet
you found each other like this this
is the way you found
each other and said

    this is
    it this
    is what I
    want I swear
    but now if
    you were
    different and I
    could be different
    then things would have to

don't say it
like that can't you
see I just need
a minute give
me a break why can't
you let it be?

(the baby   looks   from one
to the   other   says
mommy   *daddy*   *party?*

he doesn't know   a word for it yet
long tears   go down
his face he   touches
the wet patch   growing
on his coat   says *ow*)

man overboard

like a dark fish it swims to you and you
resist do not want to be consumed
but it's true and swallows you

you see out through smoke-hued
scales overlapping like breast feathers
through the gills like blood-prayers blooming

and collapsing to the beat of loss and a pulse
you find struggling out from your throat
you lean against the flesh of the fish

which possesses you and the fish does not object
it swims with purpose certain and transparent
as a long evaporation of musical notes

it contains all that you need the weeping
creates a flame and you burn there sheltered
when you tip to char a weightless curl this vessel

thins and thins and you breathe back
your regular breaths you are released lift like a
lick of weed again sweet scat in the current of the sea

steps to hell

Which step was she,
sleek as she was, blind
as a bride or a mare

in her stall, haltered,
tethered? He knew that,
with a drinker's bright eye,

yet he came on, pacing
the aisle, rattling his bucket of oats.
Here girl, and she put

a faith in him as he came
crooning *Beauty*. He
promised beyond—

the shimmying flame,
something thirsty
that admitted no end.

what should you say when he asks

naturally you wish to kill him
boil him in a pot and eat him first

the brain which thought of it
then the hands that reached for it

last the cock that finished it you want to
peel yourself just to escape the stain

of your skin so you won't feel: how
he lied by touching how you remember

every touch how he has touched you
everyplace every place he has been

divorce comedy

Closure session in counseling,
he notes, "Except, I've met someone."

She's thirteenth, a good number. Luckily,
each was a spirit sent to rescue him!

Going home he thanks you for the years
it took to overcome his distaste for breasts.

"You prepared me." Contemplative or dumb,
you do not stop the truck and make him walk.

The ending in bed, under the unfinished
ceiling and the light: nothing much happens.

The moment, if anything, is a small, gray bubble
that bobs, horribly shining, then popping with relief.

the drinkers

Shaping rough

        sculptures of big

            women he'd sing

Bird on a wire,

      you thinking he had

          an ugly voice,

reassuring as burlap.

        He offered

          those large, alluring

     hands. But there was

         something…yes, he knew

the amber place

      where food

        sickens and any lucid

    tunes twist

      like serpents in the grass.

    You stuck

  with the man

    believed to be

       clean

    but had mistaken

  the face

    of the man climbing up

        for the face of a man

    climbing down.

  Wasn't long:

you stood in the vile

                                    pasture, and

   above swung charred

                        rungs of the ladder, his

        stronger legs

                stepping up

          the blue

  and breaking

         water—

its unfamiliar will—

         and kicking away.

the wonder

how he was a terrible kisser
how he was small but you lied
and really he tasted like piss
his greasy hair swinging malodorous
and the sweat on his red swelling face
how the man drove out the man how
he stood by and let it go forward
how you loved him at all
how you loved him

white hoop

You ask *What lasts?* Listen—the rain
is stopping. Out the window, tree full of birds
like dark eyes. If the sun forgets us, something else
will come.
                    The long hair of the men
drifting across their shoulders will fill you
with happiness. It will become like the clang of
the blacksmith's hammer that slowly bends
iron to a white hoop,
                    become
as clear as these syllables
from the teacher's lips—just wetted
by the glass of water we place at her side—
as she reads what she wrote thirty years ago
about sharing the rent.
                    You were making a song of
his name to hear for the rest of your life. It is still
there. The upstairs neighbor heard someone strangling
a woman, but it was you, coming alive.
                    Where are
the dotted lines? So you can tear this life
into streamers to whip the wind, share
the long white flags with those you meet
on the road, startle the gulls, loud and
frank in their hunger, watch their knife-wings
manage the air the way we manage

                              ordinary things
like how to position two hands into a clasp. Rescue
not easy, but you can piece
something— larger, but never
indestructible. There must be
many kinds of breakwater.

2

solid

mountains

you didn't know
that even wide rivers dry up
that something wanted you

to die   that you were anything
near beautiful   you did wonder
about the huge print lost

from its trail   in stone
where it was going   in school
you learned what left it ate

the young of another species
(good friends   stop by
and you want to say *we lived*

 up there   but they're telling
where to buy the most fabulous
apples   we speak for a while

of fruit   no matter   it takes
a lot of time   you'll need a long
long time to remember)

certain moss

you are   somewhere else
by now not   where once
they thought you   weren't crying

the time   on the stairs or
time the sky   blew clouds
in procession like   cages in a zoo-train

somewhere else listening
for owls waiting out the cold as
the light goes snow up over your boots

they think   they hear you
but you're a star   no longer
in the place your light   seems to come from

past the dark barn
farther than these woods
where you started to learn names

of plants walking single
file someone   talking to you over a shoulder
fingering the common leaf

you plucked from its stem past the
hill they have called Big Trestle
under rusted wire

out past the edge   that dissolving place
where particles of light cling
to the lip of the earth

not about waiting   today or the name of a certain
moss whose spore-heads float like
tiny flames   an inch above

the green bed on filaments too fine to see
but when they turn   to the spot you
were granted to occupy

the syllables of your name ready
that is not where you are no
not where you'll be

your life has stood

no wait: then you'd see a
gun but: there was none
only the   (gun)   wish
then you   knew: you were
gunless   angry   at the blank of it
white   noise   of self   unarmed: even
the gun   idea   stolen: no   wait never a
gun to begin   with just: ungun: the child

(like a flower the antigun of her yolk imagine such)

stuffing bullets   in a brassy craw
wishing your   wish were not you
until you see   *even minutes* brim
and die like   prayers:
to dissolve   back
to the non   an un   pre
of fallen   /or/ you will   grow
forgetful   will gum   eggs
tangerines   and hours   the balloon
will arrive   with no   mind
of gun   when you un: become

we look back and see

When you were first born, your eyes
were blue and you couldn't see but what you felt
was real. In the crib you screamed against
the bars and no one came and that was knowing.
The milk pale blue from the mother's breast
shone through your new skin. A lode of fear
and hiding place of longing: what we become.
Words pressed into you. Your flesh
did not belong to you alone. There were scratches
where you tried to push your way through
the neighbor's hedge. At night you lay and
imagined the blood you'd left, telltale drops
on the property of another, his twigs and thorns.
The liberty you felt when you drank from the red
tin cup that hung by the backyard faucet on a hook:
the taste of rust like danger or sun on your tongue.
You rode your bike around the block and
the houses seemed full of boys, their soft
secret knees and hair like forgiveness, and already
you wanted to burrow into them. However high
they held it above your head, maybe
wrapped in pretty paper, you saw
what you wanted, you knew it was yours.

the pass

But other snapshots. Pike's Peak in the windshield
gleaming. Lost Man Falls steep behind you,
stones like pillows. Your hair

combed school-straight. Ski lessons: speed fear.
Balloons tugged at the porch rail. How you bit
the boy who pushed your sister till he bled,

then spat and spat along the road to get the tang
off your tongue. Then shut her in the shed for crying.
You hated the matching dresses because they matched.

You loved the godly places too. The camp.
A burning slope. Dog-tooth violets like stars
underfoot. How not to pick them.

the river

from bluffs where teenagers dug caves
where trees teetered   taproots pegging them
to the cliff-edge   fat ropes hung

you thought *someday I'll get up there*
not a pretty river   not bright or blue
gray trees lay toppled   roots and grass

packed to burlap   maybe winter   the big
kids gone   alone in the white
feet heavy as stove-lids   or it's

a dream as with a long stick you test
the snow   below it a shield of ice   and
you're digging for the locked river   the real one

the porch

You have a cereal bowl, large,
cream-colored, with a green rim,
one of the following painted on the bottom:
eggplant, head of lettuce, parsnip, pumpkin,
cucumber with a tail of vine. The gray kitten,
ears sticking out, eyes still slate-blue,
struggles onto your leg, falls off. His skull

makes a knock on the porch. He pushes
his face in the milk, sneezes, purrs: sound
of steel beads falling. Rain-colored stripes
in the dark of his fur. That is the porch
of your childhood, the green-black beetle
droning, a dirty splinter. The place you were
solid, a heat you could take for granted.

yes no

like fire kicked open
like the rodeo clown   his dirty pants
on a thorn   in a tailspin
on the pillow you couldn't smell any more
without bearing without   signal how
could you   explain your own
rage then   here came   theirs when
salt clotted   for the time   you were late
the way you   cut bread
on the escalator   under   darkness
if you ate your vegetables
if you didn't

girl who liked doors

What if you'd told them
the girl next door had a thing
for putting things in her,
you know, then in yours?
What if you had said you hated
the shaft of the doorknob,
the can-opener handle,
the key? What if you'd told Mrs.
Sharp, who made us "face out"

if we colored past the lines
and put you in the closet
the day you "told a lie"? She
liked doors: cabinet doors
to stack the nasty
paints behind, the locking
of her important rooms.
You knew the girl
your friend, didn't want

to hurt her feelings, so you tucked
the key between your legs,
that's all she wanted.
She had no words
for what you were doing, and
if you had known you had

to tell, who would you
have gone to, how would you
have started to speak?

asthma

You were most in danger then. Sick in your parents'
bed, their warm delicious musk, seeming
to you the true
smell of the universe, sheets
extra-bald from
unimaginable rubbings. Counting the snagged
threads of the old fake-
satin comforter, coughing,
sneezing or just unable to breathe, you could be
happy there. His hand on your head
or rubbing your back when lungs tightened
to hot fists. Or she brought
cups of something to drink. In the dark,
allowed to watch
the TV's white eye all day if you wished and no one
stopped you.
They brought you food
on a tray. And on that
day everyone
asked how you were.
The danger then was feeling
it was possible
for them to care for you
enough and all you had
to do was
not be able to breathe.

other girl

When she cast her hook, she pulled out a fish,
nice-sized. She killed it with the butt of her knife,
slit the belly, and with the sound of tearing emptied it

of complication. Entrails she dropped in the current
and forgot. Forever. At home, someone
fried the fish and she ate it all with pepper and salt.

The skin, the cheeks, the eyes. She went out
in a jacket too thin, did not allow
the blue hearts of tulips staring back

to disturb her. Did not play dolls, excel
in school, or cry. Didn't hate anyone or ask
why. You wanted to climb into her body

and hide, would bump against her as you
walked. She'd look sideways,
then step to place one girl-space in between.

measles

They brought mug after mug of tannin-bitter tea,
no milk, no sugar, and mostly you poured it
out the window. Downstairs Gram saw it once
go past, said nothing. They darkened the room.

No books. No TV. Your aunt came to read a long
story about trolls who dug, skidding on slagheaps,
to the root of the mountain, and found a man, stone blind,
who begged for a little wine or bread. When your eyes

were safe, they raised the shades: too much. Sun
shrieked at grass, trees bickered. When they said *Time
to go back to school*, you wished you could retreat
to the cave: tea, dry toast, the long jeweled tale of shadows.

blue torso

Clang of troughs assaulted all night
by pigs. Dangerous ram slamming in his pen.
The fallen place where you found a blue torso,
lid half of a cookie jar shaped like
a woman, the wings

of her cap flying back, hands folded like a singer's
below her breast, pressing a secret. Treasure,
you brought her to your mother after "husband"
drove off to work, wondering how many miles
the soybeans went on and what came after but corn.

The neighbor's big son came to the back door,
rubber boot full of blood. He wanted to wash
before his mother saw. Your mother tried,
she did, but the blood kept on coming.
She had no car, the baby: sent you

to walk him home. Black
bubbles of tar shone on that road in the sun.
You dreamed about him, washing and washing
his hands. The green boot smelling of hog
and spilling such a red onto the floor.

through the wall a voice

Your sister standing still as a knob, not
saying, never saying:
Why don't you ever talk about me?
The day is blank again and

through the wall a voice
fires instructions at a group,
children milling in waves
that wash against walls, crash

back, regather, hurl
themselves and this is like the tide
in your head, a sound like bullets, memory
dizzies down like a firework that goes

off by accident one October.
The tide carries you, your sister,
a white dog with bad breath, the old VW,
its upholstery smelling like a chemical,

and the sheets of Iowa
lightning that awed you apart, you
into the rain out under
the snowball bush, her to bed with her pact

of silence to keep. How could
you not see that she brimmed
with the kind of stillness
inside the barn at the center of a storm,

that her spirit the color of honey seemed
to be about contentment but was really
about waiting. What lasts
about you, cold under

the bush where dripping, heart-shaped
leaves delay the rain, is that you
are her sister. But then, you were just
a fist, curled and burning.

the body

The forgetting of that time is a long
hollow tube in your mind. Your own body
was like that cry we think we hear in the quiet
but decide must be imagined.
Spelling tests, yes, and a brass bell.

The day they called the girls out as if
you'd all been caught cheating. Into the hall,
up to the attic, no kidding, with the nurse
in her wimple-hat, to see the movie
about how when you "become a woman,"

when you "begin menstruation," you can have
a new dress, this one from the department store
where a military man holds the door open
for your mother and you. You must wash
extra. And a crinoline.

How you loved the black sheer stockings
of the teacher's aide, and the boy with half
arms, hands like flippers, with his wish
to shoot hoops. You do remember. How you shot
that ball over and over, October to May,

even in snow when the ball lost its ringing
sound like metal on the lot. Fourth grade,
you had bangs, he a buzz-cut, another girl,
none of you looking at the three-
fingered probe growing out of his shoulder

and the paddle of pronged flesh with which in the spring
he lobbed a high one, clean,
just like a dream, *swish*, and the three of you,
leaping like winners on *Let's Make a Deal*,
grabbed each other then with whatever you had.

pocket

Gray beech, some diseased.
Leaves shiver, flinch. Smell of ferns,
wintergreen, the dull and factual cold.
That final child died.

You smooth her out, fold in
the arms, roll—the size of a knobby fist.
Heavy. Ribby. You smell old vinyl, olives,
the metallic tang of dirty glass: the city

ahead. Ended in the trees,
she's soft as a cat now, light
as a cotton dress. Like a meal
in your pocket, the girl.

five fantastic ways to die

1. No Dial Tone

your mother loved you when you
looked like her with your little sun
glasses on top of your head and she called
you by mistake her name

2. God Called and You Answered

the edge of the asphalt where the red
ball rolls away and you are about
to enter the thicket of nettles when
above your head bursts a fist
of bright blue snips   butterflies
which you haven't even heard of
yet and you forget everything
everything as they rise

3. Yes

the time
the one you
wanted wanted
you and there
weren't words
just the tongue
speaking churches
confession
speaking bells

4. Return of the Prodigal

the word that fell back into place
precise triangular oiled original
space it
jolted from by accident four
centuries ago

5. Speed Time

then after that it's time then
to speed time and the seed
calls to its
name and the name
of the seed draws the word
up on its reel the word
soon invisible
the cord a blur

6. In Silence

and the end's no cut place but
a handle to lift
the pane that broke or genuflect the coffee
to the stove   things jump from frames
leaf out   or it's one
dogwood
leaf opening at the center of your eye
and when you give it the right
name it starts to smoke

3

no sequel

look up

could you refuse the stars   the sting
bringing us to the brim
we hear them

chime and cold but   the telescopic
bottomless doubt   our singular
unmattering   another fragile hour up

the cone of night   throat of nothing   they fly away
from your eyes   the hand
at your side fisted   warm   still a little uplifted

vanishing point

so you bought
portable things expensive
and cheap the way love turned
out expensive and cheap
tiny kettle, chairs to fold oven
the size of a shoebox

as if you could load a travois
call your dog and head out
could find the tribe that's gone ahead

with baptized eyes

(The gaze of) a baby empty and blue, gaze
of the watchers (who kneel at this game)
of jacks, of the lover (so sure) of the seen.
The enemy's (gaze all charcoal and) blade

or (mother-gaze feathering edges to) truce.
The gaze of brides down the long gamut,
(of grooms) up the long gamut,
salmon-gaze, white (spawn and) white water,

yours now (at how many lines) left,
our gaze (through space looking) for you,
(our gaze) at receding backs of friends,
the gaze of the (baby asking and) blue:

with silence (no possible) omissions,
with language how same (the drama),
our circle (matted) in the grass,
and whenever you (don't) speak (again)

(of love), how easily it looks on the face
(like pain). Without words how clean our (actions:
closed) (to misreading, to) lies. When you
forget (to shut the door to) peace,

does the day knock (and ask) the same
question? With your eyes do you (know
how to) answer (its call? Are you
still left holding) the chill china knob?

green

You had softened, dissolved, become but liquid
other people swam in, that you
swam in, coloring and confusing yourself.
Various others rushed by, peddling hard,
while you drifted in a thick-tongued tide of
purely green, called it failure, necessity.
Your new chant was *diapers diapers bedtime*
and *sweetheart, no.* Later, *this time she won't
come back.* You went on and on, sealike—

maybe we've been there—first fast
and uncontainable, then full of urchins
poisonous and jellyfish pumping on a current
similar to love. The hated starfish
grows back arms overnight, again
the dying, birthing, the inconceivable
vanishing of whole humans, the spark and raising,
everywhere, of new worlds, and nobody
noticing, not even, particularly, you.

You got used to it, how there was no way
to mark this passage, the self so permeated
there was no one to "be," voice transparent, large,
plain like the call of whales. How
your breath lasts now. How you miss
those gone. How you live in a river

so swift you are frightened. How no song will
replace or approximate those missing
and you must find another use for words.

tide going out

and the words look for you will find you
words   white birds through the air and the air
something you'll drink

when you're thirsty through your whole body
the sea lifts a sound to touch your face
and you let it   the contour of your cheek
the gray gentle lids of your eyes and then the words

find you and move across your tongue
cool and green as new peas   the word moves
in your mouth and the air breathes you in

you remember how a voice

supple quick   warm dives
into your ear   like a mink ripples   down
the marrow   to the solid   unshockable
    brain stem the   felted stranding
pelt of sound   stops breath:
once he   mentioned   Picasso
warped   his wives   and you were
    swimming   his mouth the riptide
of syllables   (each sea   turtle remembers
the first shore   returns   in her mind
blind whirling)   rightness)   knitting)
    up your   throat wanting
to touch   and not   but feeling
invaded   delayed   the voice

you cannot say

where it came from cannot
remember a name a
destination no

fork in the road no mainsail
oily skidmark original
sin but it

asks for
nothing eats nothing
marks no territory marvels

for no one
buried or bare it waits
intangible massive silent shrill it

moves under your hands
your breath your
glance shifts

its tint thickness
of membrane no eyes
with which to study accuse claim

waits is waiting
for a word before the lid for
you to say yes I   know you   mine

wives

When you spoke of your man they said
how terrible and you said how terrible when

they spoke of theirs. Solace in their stories,
the magnificent sameness. After the final papers,

your mother made casserole for moving day,
but none of the wives came or sent their terrible men

to help, good women who used to call often,
who said how terrible, who said poor you.

five sure-fire steps for rescue

1.

How it's done
(you know already)
no one knows. Feather-not-possible,
it flies. You say *how? how?* and hear:
the noise we make in pain.

2.

Yet pressed
like a blade along a life
pain leaves
these parts enlarged.

3.

Swollen, it returns, asking
How? How did you
survive me? Also meaning:
how did I find you, kindly host
who gave me a place
to blaze, to die?

4.

You become the vast
sky specializing in birds
and other longing.

5.

And you are the grave:
the finished, what flies.
What are the major feathers of the wing?
You will answer *Pain, our darling,*
who brought parting, knowledge, arms.

6.

What comes after
is similar to the day you were named:
open, intentioned, prone
to cherish and err.

territory alternative

a day soft
as water as wishes as
yes just broke you again

choose now the red
of tomatoes the good
green-gold seeds like

eyes in their jelly
this wealth of decay
and daylight

without spectator
salt or loss without
oh

they ask you about middle age

First the engorgement of modest
success. Then birth, the prizing away of ripened
favorites which sank

down the channel in a clotting mass.
And just loneliness. The one who said all things had
meaning turned like a bulldog

and bit. No exit but exit.
Honesty expensive now! Starch of complacency:
grateful for waiting,

for rooms, a sandwich, forced
hot air. Then the remarkable silence— vibrant, black
outer space, where we live—

made it hard to turn back.
Soft, barely believable mornings (and other sweet
fruits) do grow.

reflection in a hard surface

he said one thing   meant another   and didn't you ache
with the truth   like a hair   denied
rooted   back   into your face
was his truth   impounded
like a bad dog   (he lied)   in your eyes
a willingness   he looked
        back with meaning
      un meant   saw a you
        not you (no one) he
lied to you them us her   and the you you
thought you
were isn't   now   so   who
listened   who ate
the bait   who let it into the
ear like a drop   of warm oil did it ease
something there   where we had hardened did we
store his lie   down   in red coils did the hue of our listening
reach for him to tell it   (the story) again (the story) welcome
and annihilating did we assist did we assist weren't we there

summer

Today the sun is out which is sad.
Trees sad when rustling and when still.
Leaves that drop in July. When the lilies
open their widest, it is sad to be
alone in the house. Guests will come,
how strange to provide only foods they enjoy.
They don't know he broke chairs
across the back of the table until the table
broke. It is sad that he slept
with those women, some of whom you
also fed at that table. Discussing it,
civilized, was sad, and the climb up
again and again to start over. Today you return
from a smooth sea, laughing
at the story you did not expect, forgetting.
You think, when you feel it return,
how loyal sadness is, how accustomed you are,
spreading its folds about you.
You are clean today as if becoming old
were the long, slow purification
of lives, as if what gets called *heart* grows in later,
as if witnessing wreckage
translates it into something else, lifts an image our
own, sweep and color: loss
could be art. We might stop here. But the day
is redeemed at a price. Among the waves

you wondered what it would be not to try, not
fold the triangles or plan baking time,
be the person who didn't come up.
Wednesday and you set another table. Admiring the green
of the salad, you notice the world
had promised you nothing, has broken no vow.

your mother starts talking

I am a long curtain   I am five
    brown pears on the counter   in the sun
       I am this glass of water   cold
        the breath in your ear   ten times
      smaller than your wish   I am fire
    which creeps underground   root to root
    that girl with long hair   thick as hay
her birthday the same   as yours   I'm
   rain in warm wind   mouth   of the silo
   a yellow tile   the tortoise   dragging
     to shore   fierce-spattering   snow
  on the windshield   as you grind
  the last hill before   knowing   you are   lost
I am   a pirate feather   pope's   razor   the germ
    in your nose   I am not   the triple
crown   not ice   not bricks   stacked neatly
    not a snake   black   with yellow
diamonds   for my spine   not   the state
   Oregon   or the fog   not   sand
    that rills   and reforms   itself   across
    the Sahara   I am not   your   daughter
not your creator   not the   bleeding
    hangnail   or the needle   the doctor brings closer
   I am not lies   and not the   truth you have
been looking for   not the farmer   receiving chemo or
fender you scraped   am not the   envelope am

not nor have ever   been traffic light   bird's nest
                bottle of milk   football jersey   the smell
        of the last game still   caught up   in all those
evil little holes   I am not the   plug not
                window glass   not the   permission
                slip you forge   I am   not a bank   straddling safety
                deposit vaults   not the   city
        of Jerusalem before during or after prayer

the owl in your name

In the forest of ribs
no need to muster sky. She pulls the air behind her—
winging the breathable

world. Her job to stop
the small fast-beating ones, their twiggable limbs
and gray ribbons of fear. Their chittering
dissolves into stillness.

There's choice:
will you turn your name into the hole, all darkness
and no letters? Who would call for you
no longer if you did?

Answer it: what would yours
bring,
edible and open in her grip?

ceremony for coming of age

willing   to eat anything
to drink   the milt of salmon
take this   break open its life   we know
how step   after step   we show
you till we   come   like a Lazarus
to open water   the chandelier is made
of eyes   when skirts
trail   we tear them away   stamp
whirl   the men fall back   afraid   you laugh
shout   trample the dirt   you cling   yet to the thundering
edge   yes it's blood   and the men the men
are afraid   (who else   has gone beyond)
they believe   a fish   in its mail
lives better   than any   queen   feel the water's
silver eye   its secret   shatter: blooming
the new   pang   simple: you
see: you see: you will have   no sequel

and the others

the hair stood up on your neck
throat closed around a word
forgot to breathe remembered forgot
gut hurt back hurt memory
hurt

you heard her name
his name hers
got a drink of water
knee-balls ached couldn't take a step
someone calling a door slammed

had to stop eat cake from a box
lost hearing in one ear
particle screaming under the shore
eye higher than fear the other
life tipped a

beautiful hurtful flash
days like dirt like salvation quiet
night joy for no reason black
tide green tide
a hand from the waters

cold something bitten cut
and silence for a mouth now
far   the mind can rise
here   there a shepherd   ghost-
laugh   someone   paddling

he learns to speak

tell me the story tell it
again how does rain get
that high how can I hate you
then love you why do trees make
all that snow why aren't
you president show me
how this apple works
don't let me die the best thing
about flying is the bulldozer
below you funny how an eyeball
can't see itself what's fire
made of anyway stay
with me when I sleep and love
me some more tell it again

paradise

You arrive where the end upends, un-
braids, where the air grinds

suffering like meal. Ribbed with your wishes,
the gunwales of the craft split speed, runnels

like years curl back thick. The pleasure
of *abide*: the root: just the trip

cold / unbroken / no speech:
the meaning in all contraction:

womb our only godly
muscle: wanting what we want.

grasslands

you force the car
fast on the oiled road
narrowing like love become

useful but you
are fruitful pining
magic as a frying pan

see how
explanations pow
smear harden on the windshield

kansas
said come
dakotas sang empty is

beauty
too see the grass see
the line the line the line and all the sky

as you know do not forget

this is the picture of a saint feet
pointing down this is the bent
feather the horn in your ear this
is the edge of a lemon the foot

in the stirrup the gate
open this is the motion: shut
this was a road of cinders

this was the weather in your head
this was the tendon of leather we
are wires we are wires we are

tented up like this we are another
method we are not the eye you see we
are not the eye you use
we are the eye

below the lifeboat

If you wake up under your life, you see
the shore fall away and fade, no oars, no voice
to do your singing, no blue marble for luck,
a rumpled dollar, but so what? Something rants
in the farthering trees, from here

mere tick of motion. A sleeve of sun left:
slipping. The life you thought was yours—
you kept trying to save it—closes like water and
you can't see past flesh, can't feel your hands.
The water grows. You *want* to drift.

Then anger bigger than memory, then praise
for all you lost, then the pale and flowering
landless place and flashing fish, past
the scattered word "me," into the
rank, the translated and free.

after detour

you see: lost miles (too)
point to the mark:
your one heat:

a blue kind
bullseye:

the beat of you:
this only mind:
homing, sulfuric, unified.

about the author

Nancy White grew up bouncing around the country until adolescence, when her family settled back near its roots in Cambridge, New York. She attended Oberlin and received her MFA at Sarah Lawrence. Her first book, *Sun, Moon, Salt*, won The Washington Prize for Poetry. She serves as Associate Editor at *The Sow's Ear Poetry Review* and Editor at The Word Works in Washington DC. She teaches at Adirondack Community College, after wonderful stints at Saint Ann's School in Brooklyn and at Bennington College. Happily returned to Cambridge, New York, she lives with her husband and son, tending the same gardens her grandmother planted. She has painted the farmhouse walls red, green, yellow, blue.

Breinigsville, PA USA
06 April 2010
235621BV00001B/22/P

9 780979 668432